Truly Messianic

Become ANOINTED
and Holy Spirit EMPOWERED

DOMINIQUAE BIERMAN

Author of *The Healing Power of the Roots*

First Printing June 2024

Paperback ISBN: 978-1-953502-82-7
E-Book ISBN: 978-1-953502-83-4
Printed in the United States of America

Kad-Esh MAP Ministries
52 Tuscan Way, Ste 202-412, St Augustine, FL 32092, USA
www.Kad-Esh.org

Published by Zion's Gospel Press
shalom@zionsgospel.com
www.ZionsGospel.com

ZIONS GOSPEL
PRESS

Dedication

This book is dedicated to all those who have discovered that the Messiah is Jewish and the true Gospel came out of Zion, Israel, about 2000 years ago. It is Him who said,

> "But you will receive power when the Ruach ha-Kodesh has come upon you; and you will be My witnesses in Jerusalem, and through all Judah, and Samaria, and to the end of the earth."

Acts 1:8

CONTENTS

Introduction

MUCH HAS BEEN SAID AND written about the present-day Messianic movement that endeavors to restore the Jewish Roots of the faith. This book is not for the purpose of repeating what has already been said, but rather it is to bring the Messianic movement home to its origins - namely the 21st century like the 1st century. It is time to restore the full manifestations and workings of the Holy Spirit that have often been shunned and quenched in many Messianic circles.

The word Messianic means ANOINTED with the Holy Spirit's power to rule. We are too late in time and the days are evil. We must recover the fullness of the Holy Spirit's power that the Jewish apostles of the 1st century possessed.

> "Behold, I have given you authority to trample upon serpents and scorpions, and over all the power of the enemy; nothing will harm you."
>
> Luke 10:19

1

It is time to get rid of all the ravages of replacement theology which, among other things, replaced a Jewish Messiah for a Roman Christ and the Holy Spirit for religion.

To my Messianic and Christian brethren and co-laborers in Yeshua's vineyard: I appeal to collaborate with the Father to bring forth the full restoration of *all* things. (Acts 3:17-19)

I will call this new thrust of the Messianic movement by the term MAP (Messianic-Apostolic-Prophetic) Movement, which is now encompassing the globe. The MAP Movement is espousing a joining of Torah and Ruach, Word and Spirit, fruit and gifts, love and power. Ultimately, this will form the one new man, the bride of Messiah, Jew and Gentile grafted into the same olive tree, filled and empowered by the same Holy Spirit, worshipping the same Jewish Messiah, whose name is Yeshua. Then we will be ONE, echad, and the world will believe in Him.

> **"I pray not on behalf of these only, but also for those who believe in Me through their message. The glory that You have given to Me I have given to them, that they may be one just as We are one—"**
>
> **John 17:20, 22**

CHAPTER ONE

Glory or Ichabod?

Then she named the child Ichabod saying, "The glory has departed from Israel"—because of the capture of the ark of God, and because of her father-in-law and her husband."

1 SAMUEL 4:21

I N ANCIENT ISRAEL, THE PEOPLE knew that battles could only be won when bringing the Ark of the Covenant, which housed the presence of the living God. The enemies of Israel also knew this, and they were afraid any time the Ark showed up. However, the presence and power of Yah (God) cannot be manipulated. When the people, and especially the priesthood, were pleasing unto YHVH, then the Shekinah, His indwelling Presence, fought for Israel. But when the priesthood was corrupt, that same Shekinah turned against the corrupt priests.

"So the Philistines did fight and Israel was defeated—they fled every man to his tent. The slaughter was very great, as 30,000 of Israel's foot soldiers fell. Moreover, the ark of God was captured, and Eli's two sons Hophni and Phinehas died."

1 Samuel 4:10-11

The presence of the Holy Spirit is *light* and it exposes all sin. People cannot hide behind religion or a false image when His glorious presence shows up. That is why in the early church, which was totally Jewish, liars were exposed - like in the case of Ananias and Sapphira, who had promised an offering to the apostles and brought only part of it. They died while shamelessly lying to Peter, and the young men buried them. The healthy fear of God permeated this first covenant community where the Holy Spirit had complete freedom. This caused many to be added to their numbers. Others that were not ripe for salvation kept their distance.

> And great fear came over the whole community and all who heard these things.

Acts 5:11

The power and presence of the Holy Spirit either draw people or repel them. This is a true divider between those who are repentant and those who are religious but unrepentant.

Receiving the fullness of the Holy Spirit is a commandment given to the first Jewish disciples. They were not allowed to do anything without the power of God.

Now while staying with them, He commanded them not to leave Jerusalem, but to wait for what the Father promised—which, He said, "you heard from Me."

Acts 1:4

"But you will receive power when the Ruach ha-Kodesh (Holy Spirit) has come upon you; and you will be My witnesses in Jerusalem, and through all Judah, and Samaria, and to the end of the earth."

Acts 1:8

The absence of His Holy Spirit's power and glory is called ICHABOD. Yeshua told His Jewish disciples that without His power (His kabod/glory) they could do nothing! No good works or good intentions advance the agenda of His Kingdom without the glory and power of His Holy Spirit. All Messianic and Christian leaders who care about His Kingdom should *stop* what they are doing until they and their constituents are filled with the Holy Spirit.

Long ago, when I was in my 30's, I became a pastor in Tel Aviv and the Father gave me two words that have accompanied me in my ministry, against all odds:

1. The good is the enemy of the perfect.
2. It is better to be popular with God than with men.

Doing good works while rejecting the power and manifestation of the Holy Spirit is the enemy of true kingdom works.

> ..., holding to an outward form of godliness but denying its power. Avoid these people!
>
> 2 Timothy 3:5

Those who seek to be popular with men often shun and reject the Holy Spirit, because the Holy Spirit puts a demand on all that you do and on who you are. The Holy Spirit "messes up" our selfish and worldly plans and exposes all false motivations. You cannot be politically correct and Holy Spirit-empowered at the same time. And YES! There are plenty of politics in the Christian Church and Messianic circles.

If you desire popularity with the God of Israel, you will refuse to continue without the Holy Spirit's power and presence - just like Moses did.

> But then, he said to Him, "If Your presence does not go with me, don't let us go up from here! For how would it be known that I or your people have found favor in Your sight? Isn't it because You go with us, that distinguishes us from all the people on the face of the earth?"
>
> Exodus 33:15-16

The Holy Spirit can be grieved easily when you ignore his instructions (or rather her instructions because Spirit or Ruach in Hebrew is in feminine gender; the Ruach HaKodesh or Holy Spirit is likened unto a dove, which is also in feminine gender).

When we surrender and become fully empowered and possessed by the Holy Spirit, we become a different kind of people - a peculiar people, a people who are accountable to God for all our attitudes, thoughts, and actions. At the same time, we become fully dependent upon His grace, mercy, council, and leadership. We fully realize that without the Holy Spirit, we are nothing and we cannot do anything of value for His kingdom. We walk on this earth, but we are not of this world. We have become His possession for Him to do with us and through us whatever He pleases. Our life takes on a miracle dimension and we know we belong to Him.

> "I am the vine; you are the branches. The one who abides in Me, and I in him, bears much fruit; for apart from Me, you can do nothing."
>
> **John 15:5**

The only way to abide in Him and be one with Him is by the anointing and power of the Holy Spirit. This kind of close intimacy cannot be achieved by any religious devices or liturgies; it is only when we are *filled* with the Holy Spirit that we can be ONE with Him. And this brings about miraculous results when we pray and His power in us manifests His Kingdom. He dwells in us through His Word and Spirit. It is His Holy Spirit that writes His Word, His Torah, His commandments, and His promises in our hearts.

"If you abide in Me and My words abide in you, ask whatever you wish, and it shall be done for you."

John 15:7

Now to Him who is able to do far beyond all that we ask or imagine, by means of His power that works in us, to Him be the glory in the community of believers and in Messiah Yeshua throughout all generations forever and ever! Amen.

Ephesians 3:20-21

So, how does one get His power to work in them? How can one be filled with the Holy Spirit?

CHAPTER TWO

Ask, Seek, and Knock

*"But seek first the kingdom of God and His righteousness,
and all these things shall be added to you."*

MATTHEW 6:33

WHEN WE WANT HIM AND His kingdom above our own lives and needs, we will not be willing to go on without His Holy Spirit's presence and power. The Word of God tells us that the only thing we need to do to obtain all that He has for us is to ask, seek, and knock.

> **"Ask, and it shall be given to you. Seek, and you shall find. Knock, and it shall be opened to you."**
>
> Matthew 7:7

However, some people ask but do not obtain, especially in religious circles where the Holy Spirit has been shunned and rejected, where spiritual manifestations are put down and discouraged. This has caused many to be suspicious of any external manifestation of the Ruach, especially speaking or praying in tongues. We will deal with this extremely important subject separately, but for now let us understand that grieving, quenching, shunning, mocking, or rejecting the Holy Spirit's manifestations carries consequences, often serious consequences. It is not to be taken lightly what Yeshua said:

> "Whoever speaks a word against the Son of Man will be forgiven, but whoever speaks against the Ruach ha-Kodesh will not be forgiven, neither in this age nor in the one to come."
>
> Matthew 12:32

This was said in the context of people mocking Yeshua and accusing Him of casting out demons by Beelzebub, thus calling the Holy Spirit Beelzebub or Satan.

When any believer in Messiah speaks against the works and manifestations of the Holy Spirit, including judging, mocking, and putting down those who speak or pray in tongues, they come under God's judgment. I cannot think of a more painful judgment than the inability to receive the infilling of the Holy Spirit's fire and power.

The only way to come out from under this judgment is by true repentance, real *teshuva* (Hebrew for repentance). Those who have erred in this way out of ignorance or because they were so taught by their pastors and leaders will receive extreme covenant mercy and will be forgiven. But repentance must precede the infilling of the Holy Spirit. True repentance includes hating your sins and wanting desperately to be set free from all powerless religion, all immorality, all corruption, and all deception. It starts with *humility*.

> "When My people, over whom My Name is called, humble themselves and pray and seek My face and turn from their evil ways, then I will hear from heaven and will forgive their sin and will heal their land."
>
> 2 Chronicles 7:14

These deceptive and harmful anti-Messiah (anti-anointing) doctrines must be renounced if we are to see His kabod glory in our lives and congregations. The devil is deathly afraid of an empowered bridal community of believers who have the Torah written in their hearts and are empowered by the Holy Spirit to move in the miraculous.

> "These signs will accompany those who believe: in My name they will drive out demons; they will speak new languages; they will handle snakes; and if they drink anything deadly, it will not harm them; they will lay hands on the sick, and they will get well."
>
> Mark 16:17-18

These were Yeshua's last words before He was taken up to heaven on the Mount of Olives. Taking these last words lightly means taking Him and His will and testament lightly.

Replacing His words with man's humanistic, religious words and interpretations will cause us to incur God's judgment - and it stops revival and all Kingdom advancement. Remember that what people think are "good works" may be the exact opposite of what He says are Kingdom works.

> **Then the Lord Yeshua, after He had spoken to them, was taken up into heaven and sat down at the right hand of God. And they went out and proclaimed everywhere, the Lord working with them and confirming the word by the signs that follow.**

> **Mark 16:19-20**

When we are filled with the Holy Spirit, we manifest the power of His Kingdom wherever we go and in whatever we do. His Kingdom manifests on earth as it is in heaven. This is how Yeshua taught His Jewish disciples to pray:

> **"Therefore, pray in this way: 'Our Father in heaven, sanctified be Your name. Your kingdom come, Your will be done on earth as it is in heaven. Give us this day our daily bread. And forgive us our debts as we also have forgiven our debtors. And lead us not into temptation, but deliver us from the evil one.'**

> **Matthew 6:9-13**

In fact, He was teaching them to pray for His Holy Spirit to come upon them. His Kingdom only manifests through Spirit-empowered believers. The apostle Paul, who was a Jewish rabbi with a vast knowledge of theology, said that mere words do not advance the kingdom of God. The demonstration of the Holy Spirit's power is needed.

> "My speech and my preaching were not with persuasive words of wisdom, but in demonstration of the Spirit and of power— so that your faith would not be in the wisdom of men but in the power of God."
>
> 1 Corinthians 2:4-5

How many sermons are being preached from pulpits or Zoom meetings that have no power, no anointing, and do not demonstrate His Kingdom? Paul had all the theology he wanted, but He said our faith must be based on Yah's power to bring transformation, healing, and deliverance, not on the eloquent sermons of learned preachers.

Have you lost His power? Have you ever had it?

How do we go about recovering His power so we can recover His Kingdom authority?

CHAPTER THREE

Childlike Faith

*...and said, "Amen, I tell you, unless you turn and become
like children, you shall never enter the kingdom of heaven.
Whoever then shall humble himself like this child, this one is
the greatest in the kingdom of heaven."*

MATTHEW 18:3-4

WHEN WE HUMBLE OURSELVES TO seek His Holy
Spirit's power, desiring His kingdom manifestation
above our religious reasoning and self-centered motivations,
we are positioned to receive. When we are positioned to
receive, we do not tell Yah what to do or how to do it. We
just trust Him that He knows how to answer our prayers and
satisfy our seeking and repentant hearts. Childlike faith is
mandatory to see the kingdom in operation.

Too many believers are actually unbelievers and are not
willing to receive whatever God wants to give them. They

are afraid that they will lose control over their lives, or that Yah will demand something from them that they do not want to do. Others who have been indoctrinated against praying in tongues are afraid of it as if it is "of the devil" or it's "not Messianic". All of these attitudes grieve the Holy Spirit, and it is likened unto superstitious fears. We need childlike faith if we are to receive the infilling or baptism in the Holy Spirit. The first-century community of believers deemed it so important that the Jewish apostles traveled extensively to administer the Holy Spirit to new believers in the Messiah.

> **While Apollos was at Corinth, Paul traveled through the upper region and came to Ephesus. He found some disciples and said to them, "Did you receive the Ruach ha-Kodesh when you believed?" They replied to him, "No, we've never even heard that there is a Ruach ha-Kodesh."**
>
> **Acts 19:1-2**

Maybe you are like them and you have never heard, or maybe you have been indoctrinated against receiving the Holy Spirit. But I can assure you that you will be changed into another man or woman when the Holy Spirit comes upon you. This is not a psychological trick of self-persuasion or auto-suggestion; this is truly receiving the power of the Creator of heaven and earth, His very presence.

> **And when Paul laid hands upon them, the Ruach ha-Kodesh came upon them, and they began**

speaking in tongues and prophesying.

Acts 19:6

When Paul laid hands on them, two clear manifestations occurred:

1. They spoke in tongues.
2. They prophesied.

These two manifestations have always been present when new believers get filled with the Holy Spirit.

> They were all filled with the Ruach ha-Kodesh and began to speak in other tongues as the Ruach enabled them to speak out.

Acts 2:4

> "But this is what was spoken about through the prophet Joel: 'And it shall be in the last days,' says God, 'that I will pour out My Ruach on all flesh. Your sons and your daughters shall prophesy, your young men shall see visions, and your old men shall dream dreams. Even on My slaves, male and female, I will pour out My Ruach in those days, and they shall prophesy.'"

Acts 2:16-18

But what is speaking in tongues - and why is it that so many Baptist and other evangelical preachers, (Messianic included) have taught against it in the worst ways? And in the best case have taken it lightly and given it no importance? The infilling of the Holy Spirit, with speaking in tongues and prophesying, is a matter of life and death to our faith and to the lives of millions of others we could be assigned to touch. We cannot be filled with unshaken faith or unconditional love without Him. In the book of Jude, we are seriously admonished about this.

> **But you, loved ones, continue building yourselves up on your most holy faith, praying in the Ruach ha-Kodesh. Keep yourselves in the love of God, eagerly waiting for the mercy of our Lord Yeshua the Messiah that leads to eternal life.**
>
> **Judah (Jude) 1:20-21**

Judah said this in the context of fleeing ungodliness, immorality, corruption, lovelessness, and deception, all of which are running rampant today in many churches and congregations, from the biggest mega-evangelical churches to Catholic churches and even Messianic congregations. He said that in order to build ourselves up in faith and love we must pray in the Holy Spirit. Praying in the Holy Spirit is praying in tongues. These tongues are heavenly and angelic languages that are given to us when we are filled by the Holy Spirit. When we pray in these heavenly languages, we keep on building up our faith and our ability to love unconditionally. This happens miraculously when we pray in tongues and no manner of human device can cause this to happen.

The apostle Paul needed all the faith and love he could muster to preach the Good News under persecution, so he prayed in tongues a great deal more than most!

"I thank God that I speak in tongues more than all of you."

1 Corinthians 14:18

Both speaking in tongues (unknown heavenly languages) and prophesying (speaking from God in known human languages) are needed. That is why we receive both of these manifestations of the Spirit when we receive His infilling. Speaking or praying in unknown tongues builds us up personally while prophesying in a known human tongue builds others up.

It is like one of the two greatest commandments, stating to "Love your neighbor as yourself". If we do not love ourselves, we cannot love our neighbor. If we are not built up in our faith and love praying in tongues, we cannot have an anointed prophetic ministry to bless others. This is what Paul meant in the following scriptures, which have been twisted and distorted by countless preachers who have discouraged and even forbidden their members from speaking in tongues. This has grieved the Holy Spirit and has stunted the growth of millions who are faltering in their faith and are unable to walk as holy vessels or in unconditional love.

For one who speaks in a tongue speaks not to people but to God—for no one understands, but in the Ruach, he speaks mysteries. But one who prophesies speaks to people for building up, urging on, and uplifting. One who speaks in a

tongue builds up himself, but one who prophesies builds up the community. Now I want you all to speak in tongues, but even more that you would prophesy. One who prophesies is greater than one who speaks in tongues—unless he interprets, so that the community may be built up.

1 Corinthians 14:2-5

The rejection of praying in tongues has caused many to lead a powerless, backslidden, rigid, religious, and even bitter life. There is *no replacement* for praying in tongues to build yourself up in faith, holiness, and love! From that place, you can prophesy and build others up!

When you want to help someone, begin to pray in tongues first. Build yourself up in faith and love - then you will get the mind of Yah and will be able to prophesy accurately. Paul wanted all to build themselves up by praying in tongues. He did not want them to be selfish about it, but rather to give faith and love to others through prophesying. It is obvious that, if we are not connected to the power of the Holy Spirit through praying in tongues, we will not be able to give prophetically from an "empty tank". When you put gasoline in the tank of your car it is not for the sake of the car to be parked, enjoying its full gas tank. It is for you to drive the car somewhere! In the same way, when you pray in tongues you get your spiritual tank filled with fuel so you can go somewhere - to minister, prophesy, and bring salvation and healing.

> "But you will receive power when the Ruach ha-Kodesh has come upon you; and you will be My witnesses in Jerusalem, and through all Judah, and Samaria, and to the end of the earth."

> Acts 1:8 TLV

How many times have you heard at the start of a flight to put your seat belt on yourself *first* before you help your dependents? Or to put the oxygen mask on yourself *first* before you help others? Praying in the Holy Spirit, which is praying in unknown tongues, operates under the same principle: get yourself spiritually filled and energized *first*, then reach out to others with Yah's love and power. That is why Yeshua said to His disciples that *after* the Holy Spirit comes upon them, they will spread the Good News from Jerusalem to the ends of the earth.

This is also why He breathed the Holy Spirit on them when He commissioned them.

> Yeshua said to them again, "Shalom aleichem! As the Father has sent Me, I also send you." And after He said this, He breathed on them. And He said to them, "Receive the Ruach ha-Kodesh!"

> John 20:21-22 TLV

This is why Judah admonished us to stay built up in the Holy Spirit by praying in tongues. This is also why Paul wanted all to speak in tongues and prophesy, and why he himself spoke in tongues "more than all of them"- because he also prophesied and ministered salvation and miracles more than all of them. It goes together, praying in tongues and prophesying, being filled with the Holy Spirit and walking in love and power.

Are you ready to get filled with the Holy Spirit and receive heavenly languages and the ability to prophesy? Are you ready to be powerful in your faith and effective in His kingdom?

If you say YES, then pray with me:

Heavenly Father, thank You for not leaving me powerless on this earth against sin and evil. You have sent Your Holy Spirit as You promised. I position myself as a child to receive from You. Fill me with Your Holy Spirit and fire and give me Your heavenly language and spirit of prophecy. Let Your kingdom come, and Your will be done in my life on earth as it is in heaven. I praise You in advance for answering my prayer. In Yeshua's name. Amen.

Now just wait upon Him and praise Him, without self-effort, in full surrender to His presence. Be thankful in your heart that you are receiving. He may show you that you must get rid of some sin in your life that is obstructing you. Do it promptly and you *will* receive it.

> "For this reason I say to you, whatever you pray and ask, believe that you have received it, and it will be yours. Whenever you stand praying, if you have anything against anyone, forgive him, so that your Father in heaven may also forgive you your transgressions."
>
> **Mark 11:24-25 TLV**

CHAPTER FOUR

The Spirit of Prophecy

Then I fell down at his feet and worshiped him. But he said to me, "See that you do not do that—for I am only a fellow servant with you and your brothers and sisters who hold to the testimony of Yeshua. Worship God! For the testimony of Yeshua is the Spirit of Prophesy."

REVELATION 19:10

HOW DO WE KNOW THAT Yeshua is present? It is when the Spirit of Prophecy is flowing from His people. When the prophets go silent and there is no prophetic anointing in our lives and our prayers, we become dry, rigid, and religious. We go astray and begin to confuse our own opinions for Yah's will. When believers begin to figure out what Yah is saying and doing, it is obvious that we have compromised the Spirit of Prophecy. When the Holy Spirit fills us, everything we do has a touch of the prophetic. Often, we find ourselves doing and saying things we did not know because the Spirit of Prophecy flows through us.

Whatever quenches the Holy Spirit will cause the Spirit of Prophecy to run dry in us. The following is a partial list of that which grieves the Holy Spirit and will cause us to run dry:

- Compromise and lukewarmth
- Unbelief and doubting His word
- Pride and arrogance
- Unforgiveness and bitterness
- Fear of failure
- Self-righteousness
- Fear of losing control of our lives
- Rejecting or criticizing those who speak in tongues
- "Figuring out" Yah's will
- Being opinionated based on our own understanding
- Loving religious traditions more than Yah's Presence
- A judgmental spirit
- Disobedience to the Holy Spirit
- Self-preservation instead of self-denial
- Pagan traditions inherited from our ancestors, (pagan feasts replacing Biblical feasts)
- Antisemitism
- Tiredness, fatigue, and exhaustion
- Exaggerated grief and mourning with hopelessness
- Frustration
- Disappointments and self-pity
- Shunning and rejecting God's laws
- Willful sin (pornography, fornication, adultery, theft-including withholding tithes, stinginess, conniving,

addictions, abortions, rage, and more)
- Strife and quarrelsomeness
- Lying and breaking your word

The above is by no means an exhaustive list. Below are some scriptures that support this listing. Please note that there are many more scriptures; this is only a sample.

> "Do not quench the Spirit, do not despise prophetic messages, but test all things, hold fast to what is good,"
>
> 1 Thessalonians 5:19-21

Pride:

> But He gives greater grace. Therefore it says, "God opposes the proud, but gives grace to the humble." Therefore submit to God. But resist the devil and he will flee from you. Draw near to God, and He will draw near to you. Cleanse your hands, you sinners, and purify your hearts, you double-minded!"
>
> James 4:6-8

Lawlessness:

> "One who turns his ear from hearing Torah (God's laws and commandments) —even his prayer is an abomination."
>
> Proverbs 28:9

Worldliness:

> You adulteresses! Don't you know that friendship with the world is enmity with God? Therefore, whoever wishes to be a friend of the world makes himself an enemy of God. Or do you think that in vain the Scripture says, "He yearns jealously over the spirit which He made to dwell in us"?
>
> Jacob 4:4, 5

Pagan traditions:

> Thus says Adonai: "Do not learn the way of the nations or be frightened by signs of the heavens— though the nations are terrified by them. The customs of the peoples are useless: it is just a tree cut from the forest, the work of the hands of a craftsman with a chisel. They decorate it with silver and gold, and fasten it with hammer and nails so it won't totter. *(The Christmas tree is a pagan tradition)*. Like a scarecrow in a cucumber garden, their idols cannot speak. They must be carried because they cannot walk! Do not fear them for they can do no harm —nor do any good."
>
> Jeremiah 10:2-5

Antisemitism:

> But if some of the branches were broken off and you—being a wild olive—were grafted in among them and became a partaker of the root of the olive tree with its richness, do not boast against the branches. But if you do boast, it is not you who support the root but the root supports you. You will say then, "Branches were broken off so that I might be grafted in." True enough. They were broken off because of unbelief, and you stand by faith. Do not be arrogant, but fear— for if God did not spare the natural branches, neither will He spare you.

> Romanas 11:17-21

Unforgiveness and bitterness:

> "Pursue shalom with everyone, and the holiness without which no one will see the Lord. See to it that no one falls short of the grace of God, and see to it that no bitter root springs up and causes trouble, and by it many be defiled. Also see to it that there is no immoral or godless person—like Esau, who sold his birthright for one meal."

> Hebrew 12:14-16

Lying and breaking your word:

"But let your word 'Yes' be 'Yes' and your 'No,' 'No'—anything more than this is from the evil one."

Matthew 5:37

Rage and unholy anger:

"You have heard it was said to those of old, 'You shall not murder, and whoever commits murder shall be subject to judgment.' But I tell you that everyone who is angry with his brother shall be subject to judgment. And whoever says to his brother, 'Raca' shall be subject to the council; and whoever says, 'You fool!' shall be subject to fiery Gehenna. Therefore, if you are presenting your offering upon the altar, and there remember that your brother has something against you, leave your offering there before the altar and go. First be reconciled to your brother, and then come and present your offering."

Matthew 5:21-23

Lust:

"You have heard that it was said, 'You shall not commit adultery.' But I tell you that everyone who looks upon a woman to lust after her has already committed adultery with her in his heart. And if your right eye causes you to stumble, gouge it out and throw it away! It is better for you that one part of your body should be destroyed, than that your whole body be thrown into Gehenna. And if your right hand causes you to stumble, cut it off and throw it away! It is better for you that one part of your body should be destroyed, than that your whole body go into Gehenna."

Matthew 5:27-30

Immorality:

Or don't you know that the unrighteous will not inherit the kingdom of God? Don't be deceived! The sexually immoral, idolaters, adulterers, those who practice homosexuality, thieves, the greedy, drunkards, slanderers, swindlers—none of these will inherit the kingdom of God. That is what some of you were—but you were washed, you were made holy, you were set right in the name of the Lord Yeshua the Messiah and by the Ruach of our God."

1 Corinthians 6:9-11

Withholding tithes and offerings:

"From the days of your ancestors you have turned aside from My statutes, and have not kept them. Return to Me, and I will return to you," says Adonai-Tzva'ot. Yet you say: "How should we return?" "Will a man rob God? For you are robbing Me!"

But you say: "How have we robbed You?" "In the tithe and the offering. You have been cursed with the curse, yet you keep robbing Me—the whole nation! Bring the whole tithe into the storehouse. Then there will be food in My House. Now test Me in this"—says Adonai-Tzva'ot—"if I will not open for you the windows of heaven, and pour out blessing for you, until no one is without enough. I will rebuke the devouring pest for you, so it will not destroy the fruit of your land, nor will your vine be barren in the field," Adonai-Tzva'ot says."

Malachi 3:7-11

Lukewarmth:

"I know your deeds, that you are neither cold nor hot. Oh, that you were either cold or hot! So because you are lukewarm, and neither cold nor hot, I am about to spew you out of My mouth. For you say, 'I am rich, I have made myself wealthy, and I need nothing.' But you do not know that you are miserable and pitiable and poor and blind and naked. I advise you to buy from Me gold refined by fire so that you may be rich, and white clothes so that you may dress yourself and so the shame of your nakedness will not be revealed, and eye salve to anoint your eyes so that you may see. Those whom I love, I rebuke and discipline. Therefore, be zealous and repent."

Revelation 3:15-19

A Prayer of Repentance for Quenching His Spirit - Pray it out loud:

"Who can discern his errors? Cleanse me of hidden faults. Also keep Your servant from willful sins. May they not have dominion over me. Then I will be blameless, free from great transgression. May the words of my mouth and the meditation of my heart be acceptable before You, Adonai, my Rock and my Redeemer."

Psalms 19:13-15

We cannot stay clean and walk holy when we quench the Spirit of Prophecy:

For what was impossible for the Torah—since it was weakened on account of the flesh—God has done. Sending His own Son in the likeness of sinful flesh and as a sin offering, He condemned sin in the flesh— so that the requirement of the Torah might be fulfilled in us, who do not walk according to the flesh but according to the Ruach (Spirit). For those who live according to the flesh set their minds on the things of the flesh, but those who live according to the Ruach set their minds on the things of the

31

Ruach. For the mindset of the flesh is death, but the mindset of the Ruach is life and shalom. For the mindset of the flesh is hostile toward God, for it does not submit itself to the law of God—for it cannot. So those who are in the flesh cannot please God. However, you are not in the flesh but in the Ruach—if indeed the Ruach Elohim dwells in you. Now if anyone does not have the Ruach of Messiah, he does not belong to Him. But if Messiah is in you, though the body is dead because of sin, yet the Spirit is alive because of righteousness. And if the Ruach of the One who raised Yeshua from the dead dwells in you, the One who raised Messiah Yeshua from the dead will also give life to your mortal bodies through His Ruach who dwells in you. So then, brothers and sisters, we do not owe anything to the flesh, to live according to the flesh. For if you live according to the flesh, you must die; but if by the Ruach you put to death the deeds of the body, you shall live.

Romans 8:3-13

There is no way for us to submit to Elohim's commandments and ways unless we are filled with His Spirit. When His Spirit of Prophecy has freedom in us through our surrender to the Spirit, then we can walk holy by the power of His Spirit. Countless Christians and Messianics alike lead powerless lives and are steeped in sin because they have not surrendered to be filled by His Spirit. Often, it is rejecting the Spirit's manifestations of praying in tongues, singing in tongues, and prophesying that keep Christians and Messianics in bondage to sin.

> For all who are led by the Ruach Elohim, these are sons of God. For you did not receive the spirit of slavery to fall again into fear; rather, you received the Spirit of adoption, by whom we cry, "Abba! Father!" The Ruach Himself bears witness with our spirit that we are children of God. And if children, also heirs—heirs of God and joint-heirs with Messiah—if indeed we suffer with Him so that we may also be glorified with Him.
>
> Romans 8:14-17

We are led by the Spirit only when we have surrendered to the Holy Spirit unconditionally. Then we are not led by religious fear, opinions, traditions, or fleshly fervor, but are led by the Holy Spirit, who writes God's will, ways, and commandments in our hearts. Leading powerless religious lives is a great offense before the God of Israel, who paid the highest price for us to be filled with His Holy Spirit - the life of His Jewish Son and Messiah Yeshua.

We are to avoid those who are religious and pretend to be godly but deny the power of the Holy Spirit, whether with their words or actions.

> But understand this, that in the last days hard times will come— for people will be lovers of self, lovers of money, boastful, arrogant, blasphemers,

33

disobedient to parents, ungrateful, unholy, hardhearted, unforgiving, backbiting, without self-control, brutal, hating what is good, treacherous, reckless, conceited, lovers of pleasure rather than lovers of God, holding to an outward form of godliness but denying its power. Avoid these people!

2 Timothy 3:1-5

The power of the Holy Spirit is the Spirit of Prophecy, and the Spirit of Prophecy is the testimony of His Son.

Then I fell down at his feet and worshiped him. But he said to me, "See that you do not do that—for I am only a fellow servant with you and your brothers and sisters who hold to the testimony of Yeshua. Worship God! For the testimony of Yeshua is the Spirit of Prophesy."

Revelation 19:10

We can only prophesy according to our faith. When we are steeped in unbelief, the Spirit of Prophecy, (who also leads us to do Yah's will and help us in our walk) will not flow. To maintain ourselves in the faith required for us to flow in the prophetic, hear His voice, lead holy lives, and be led by His Spirit, we must pray in the Spirit - that is, pray and worship in tongues. Doing so rids us of unbelief, fear, and confusion.

But you, loved ones, ought to remember the words previously proclaimed by the emissaries of our Lord

Yeshua the Messiah— how they kept telling you, "In the last time there will be scoffers, following after their own ungodly desires." These are the ones who cause divisions—worldly-minded, not having the Ruach. But you, loved ones, continue building yourselves up on your most holy faith, praying in the Ruach ha-Kodesh (Holy Spirit). Keep yourselves in the love of God, eagerly waiting for the mercy of our Lord Yeshua the Messiah that leads to eternal life.

Jude 1:17-21

There is no other way to pray in the Holy Spirit except to pray in tongues. That is why Satan has deceived so many. It is time to repent, do teshuva, and return to the original faith as handed down to us by the Jewish apostles 2000 years ago. We are called to surrender fully to Yah's Holy Spirit, the Spirit of Prophecy, which enables us to walk holy, powerfully, and testify of Yeshua.

A PRAYER:

Yes, Abba, I return to the original gospel and the original baptism in the Holy Spirit, the Spirit of Prophecy as you gave to the original Jewish apostles and disciples. I repent for being dry and compromising Your power, replacing it with religion, traditions, and self-preservation. I humble myself and fully surrender to the Spirit of Prophecy, in Yeshua's Name. Amen.

CHAPTER FIVE

Restoring the Gifts of the Spirit

THE HOLY SPIRIT IS YAH (God) Himself and He comes with gifts and talents that are divine endowments. When we are filled with His Ruach and are born again of the Spirit, we receive gifts. Yah is the gift giver. He is the Father of lights and He always gives us good gifts.

> Every good gift and every perfect gift is from above, coming down from the Father of lights, with whom there is no variation or shifting shadow.
>
> James 1:17

The gifts that He gives are ours forever. He does not take them back, even when we turn our back on Him. He never changes His mind.

> For the gifts and the calling of God are irrevocable.
>
> Romans 11:29

In 1 Corinthians 12, there is a full list of His gifts or rather categories of gifts. These are divine abilities given to us mere humans by our loving Heavenly Father. His purpose is that we will use His endowments to help and bless others and to advance His kingdom. In order to unwrap these gifts and use them, we need faith, and we need to dispel ignorance.

> **Now concerning spiritual gifts, brothers and sisters, I do not want you to be ignorant.**
>
> **1 Corinthians 12:1**

Yah does not want us to be ignorant about these supernatural endowments. He even mentions that when we were in the world, we used to be attracted to spiritual things from the kingdom of darkness, such as divination, witchcraft, and all the occult and new-age spiritual practices. We are created to be filled spiritually and to be full of divine abilities. Satan knows that and that is why psychic hotlines and readings are thriving. But that is idolatry and an imitation of the real thing that God has for His children.

> **You know that when you were pagans, you were enticed by idols that cannot speak, and you got led astray. Therefore, I make known to you that no one speaking by the Ruach Elohim says, "Yeshua be cursed," and no one can say, "Yeshua is Lord," except by the Ruach ha-Kodesh.**
>
> **1 Corinthians 12:2-3**

People should be able to be helped supernaturally by the gifts of the Spirit operating in their lives instead of going to witches, mediums, astrologers, warlocks, and the like. Unfortunately, most of the church is powerless and dry because of ignorance, sin, and unbelief. And the gifts of the Ruach are either dormant or non-existent since we do not desire them. The arms of our Abba are full of gifts and powerful talents that no one seems to want. He must feel very sad about this state of affairs, and time is short. We must ask and receive from Him every good gift to help and bless others and bring His kingdom down to earth as it is in heaven.

Are you ready to receive, to unwrap, and to give? Are you ready to flow in His power and anointing? Then you must eagerly, passionately desire spiritual gifts. You must want them more than money, as no money can buy them.

Pursue love and eagerly desire spiritual gifts, but especially that you may prophesy.

1 Corinthians 14:1

You must desire them more than your profession, agenda, or plans. When you display His supernatural abilities, you become His vessel, His agent of guidance, instruction, healing, and deliverance.

Now there are various kinds of gifts, but the same Ruach. There are various kinds of service, but the same Lord. There are various kinds of working, but

the same God who works all things in all people.

1 Corinthians 12:4-6

Though there are many gifts and manifestations of His Spirit, there is not one person who has them all. Every person is outfitted with what is needed for his or her calling. We need each other!

> For to one is given through the Ruach a word of wisdom, to another a word of knowledge according to the same Ruach, to another faith by the same Ruach, to another gifts of healings by the one Ruach, to another workings of miracles, to another prophecy, to another discerning of spirits, to another different kinds of tongues, to another the interpretation of tongues.

1 Corinthians 12:8-10

Some people have only one gift and others have several. It is Abba who distributes them as He wills - though we can ask Him for more.

> But one and the same Ruach activates all these things, distributing to each person individually as He wills.

1 Corinthians 12:11

He both distributes His gifts among us and also *activates* them.

Pray with me:

Abba Father, thank you for the gifts of your Ruach. I eagerly desire them. Holy Spirit, please activate Your gifts in me. Enable me to operate in Your gifts to display Your kingdom to others, to reach people for salvation, to set the demon-possessed and oppressed free, to heal the sick, to mend the brokenhearted, to raise the dead, to open blind eyes and deaf ears, to guide and instruct the ignorant in your ways, and may all this be for Your Glory. In Yeshua's Name, I pray and I receive. Amen.

He (Yeshua) told them, "Go into all the world and proclaim the Good News to every creature. He who believes and is immersed shall be saved, but he who does not believe shall be condemned. These signs will accompany those who believe: in My name they will drive out demons; they will speak new languages; they will handle snakes; and if they drink anything deadly, it will not harm them; they will lay hands on the sick, and they will get well."

Mark 16:15-18

Most of His people have not been activated in the gifts of the Spirit. The reason for this is that the five-fold ministry, the chosen ministers that are supposed to be equipping the believers, are not doing their work. Either they are not in their positions and are pursuing their own lives, or they are compromised with lukewarmth, sin, and political correctness.

Many have quit the ministry, and many ministers are so dry that they buy their sermons and download them from the internet for a fee. Others are looking at ministering as a "profession" instead of a sacrificial divine call. The outcome of this is distressful! People are not equipped and trained in the gifts of the Spirit and the body of Messiah is disjointed. Many ministers have turned into interviewers and journalists instead of preachers, teachers, and equippers!

> **And He gave some as apostles, and some as prophets, and some as evangelists, and some as pastors and teachers, for the equipping of the saints for the work of service, to the building up of the body of Messiah; until we all attain to the unity of the faith, and of the knowledge of the Son of God, to a mature man, to the measure of the stature which belongs to the fullness of Messiah.**
>
> Ephesians 4:11-13 STB

Apostles, Prophets, Evangelists, Pastors, and Teachers: where are you?

Today, we have journalists, broadcasters, motivational speakers, and professional pastors and musicians - not necessarily anointed, divinely inspired, and empowered, but they are professional. They are full of knowledge of the news, politics, and philosophy, but with very little knowledge of God. Thus, the believers are not equipped to minister in the Holy Spirit. This must change lest darkness fully overtakes us! We cannot live in Messiah and not be anointed and activated to do the works of service that come with the gifts of the Spirit. His gifts are for *all* believers, not only for ordained ministers.

Apostles need to train others to go and display kingdom government, opening new territory and planting new works - accompanied by signs, wonders, and miracles.

Prophets need to activate others to prophecy and to move in the gifts of the Spirit.

Evangelists need to equip others to preach the good news of Yeshua and to display His power to heal.

Pastors need to teach others to disciple new believers and to help them in their walk in the Messiah.

Teachers need to teach others to study the Scriptures, anointed by the Spirit of Prophecy, helping them to be released in delivering His Word.

There is no alternative way to equip and empower His body except by having the five-fold ministry mentioned above fully operational. Too many ministers nowadays are not anointed, empowered, or called. I am calling anyone who is called to the ministry to come forth and report for duty! Relinquish your own life and plans and report for duty. With careful prayer, ask the Holy Spirit to connect you with a ministry that can build you up in your calling. Too many are disjointed; they are orphans, having no spiritual father or mother. If that is you, knowing you have a call and yet not knowing how to go about it, we invite you to connect with us. You will be mentored, discipled, equipped, activated, and released to operate in the gifts of the Spirit.

"The Ruach Adonai Elohim is on me because Adonai has anointed me to proclaim Good News to the poor. He has sent me to bind up the brokenhearted, to proclaim liberty to the captives, and the opening of the prison to those who are bound,"

Isaiah 61:1

Our Resouces

Visit our websites and follow us on social media

United Nations for Israel

Take a stand for the restoration of Israel and transform your nation into a sheep nation, one person at a time. Become a member and join our monthly members' online conferences to get equipped!
www.UnitedNationsForIsrael.org
info@unitednationsforisrael.org

Israel Tours

Travel through Israel with our "Bible Schools on Wheels" and watch the Hebrew Holy Scriptures come alive.
www.kad-esh.org/tours-and-events

Global Revival MAP (GRM) Israeli Bible Institute

Take the most comprehensive video Bible school online
that focuses on the restoration of all things.

www.GRMBibleInstitute.com

info@grmbibleinstitute.com

Global Re-Education Initiative
(GRI) Against Anti-Semitism

Discover the Jewish Messiah and defeat religious anti-Semitism!
Order *The Identity Theft* and GRI Online Course Package

www.Against-Antisemitism.com

info@against-antisemitism.com

From Israel to the Nations TV Programs

Watch Archbishop Dominiquae Bierman's TV programs taped
in the land of Israel!

Roku Channel: **Israel Revival**

YouTube: **Dominiquae Bierman TV**

www.youtube.com/@DominiquaeBiermanTV

Rumble: **Dominiquae Bierman TV**

www.rumble.com/c/DominiquaeBiermanTV

Broadcasting Schedule: **www.kad-esh.org/broadcasting-schedule**

MAP Prison Ministry

Through our prison ministry, pioneered by Rabbi Baruch
Bierman, GRM Bible School is studied in prisons all over the USA.
For more information & to support:

www.zionsgospel.com/map-prison-ministry/

Outlaw public display of Swastikas, Nazi and Hamas flags
www.change.org/BanNeoNazism-Evil-Can-Be-Stopped

For more information about the founder of the ministries:
www.DominiquaeBierman.com

Books & Music
For more books by Dr. Dominiquae Bierman,
order online: **www.ZionsGospel.com**

The Israel Factor
Why October 7th happened, who Hamas really is,
and why a Palestinian State is not a solution but a deception.

The Voice of These Ashes
What are the Ashes of the Exterminated Jewish People Crying For?

The Identity Theft
The Return of the 1st Century Messiah

"Yes!"
The Dramatic Life Story of an Israeli Woman who Falls
and Rises Again Because of one Word: "YES!"

Restoring the Glory – Volume I: The Original Way
The Ancient Paths Rediscovered

The MAP Revolution (free E-book)
Exposing Theologies that Obstruct the Bride

Eradicating the Cancer of Religion
Hint: All People Have It!

The Healing Power of the Roots
It's a Matter of Life and Death!

Grafted In
It's Time to Return to Greatness!

Sheep Nations
It's Time to Take the Nations!

Yeshua is the Name
The Important Restoration of the True Name of the Messiah!

The Key of Abraham
The Blessing or the Curse?

Stormy Weather
Judgment Has Begun and Revival is Knocking at the Doors!

Restoration of Holy Giving
Releasing the True 1,000-Fold Blessing

The Bible Cure for Africa and the Nations
The Key to the Restoration of all Africa

Vision Negev
The Awesome Restoration of the Sephardic Jews!

Defeating Depression
This Book is a Kiss from Heaven!

From Sickology to a Healthy Logic
The Product of 18 Years Walking Through Psychiatric Hospitals

Addicts Turning to God
The Biblical Way to Handle Addicts & Addictions

Let's Get Healthy, Saints!
The Biblical Guide to Health

The Woman Factor: Freedom from Womanophobia
by Rabbi Baruch Bierman with Dominiquae Bierman

The Spider That Survived Hurricane Irma (free E-book)
God's Call for America to Repent

The Revival of the Third Day (free E-book)
The Return to Yeshua the Jewish Messiah

Tribute to the Jew in You Music Book
Notes for the Tribute to the Jew in You Music Album

Music Albums
Abba Shebashamayim

Uru

Retorno

The Key of Abraham

Tribute to the Jew in You

Tribute to the Jew in You Instrumental

Teaching Series
God of Shalom

Israel in the War Series

The Powerful Women of the Bible

Support the Mission

Contact Us

Dr. Dominiquae & Rabbi Baruch Bierman

www.ZionsGospel.com | shalom@zionsgospel.com

Kad-Esh MAP Ministries

www.kad-esh.org | info@kad-esh.org

United Nations for Israel

www.unitednationsforisrael.org

info@unitednationsforisrael.org

52 Tuscan Way, Ste 202-412, St. Augustine,

Florida 32092, USA

+1-972-301-7087